THE ROSS AND MONMOUTH RAILWAY

The Ross and Monmouth Railway

Edited and revised by
CELIA GLOVER

BREWIN BOOKS

Published by
Brewin Books, Studley, Warwickshire.
May 1994

ISBN 1 85858 035 8

British Library Cataloguing in Publication Data.
A Catalogue record for this book is available
from the British Library.

Typeset in Press Roman and
made and printed in Great Britain
by Supaprint (Redditch) Ltd., Redditch, Worcs.

The Ross and Monmouth Railway

Repeated requests for copies of the book originally researched and written by Mark Glover when he was only twelve years old has prompted this revised and extended edition. However this revision has been undertaken by Mark's mother Celia, as Mark is now a Chartered Electronic Engineer working with railway safety systems and apart from a demanding work schedule in this country, his work takes him abroad to Europe and the Far East leaving him little time for literary pursuits!

In the preface to the two previous editions is the following quotation from one of the line's first campaigners c. 1831

"The Forest of Dean on its West side has no outlet Northwards for
its vast mineral produce but which the Ross and Monmouth Railway
would supply and as regards to passenger accommodation I can
hardly conceive a more convenient Railway".

INTRODUCTION

This book is a reminder of one of the many small railway lines that covered our country in past years. They provided jobs and happiness for many people but most were closed under Beeching's Plans. The Ross and Monmouth Railway was one of the unfortunate victims but the memory of this attractive Line is still very much alive in many peoples' minds.

The Railway joined two market towns, each having a fascinating history. When the Railway departed it had added a great deal more interesting history to both towns. Many of the old railwaymen took up new jobs and some had to move away from their home town to find work but the Railway left a great impression on them as well as the towns and villages along the route.

It is to be hoped that you will find the book as interesting as researching it was.

ACKNOWLEDGEMENTS

The Authors wish to thank - the Ross Gazette, especially former Reporters Messrs. Martin Morris and Nigel Heins, Ross-on-Wye Library, Hereford County Library, The Public Records Office, The Railway Magazine, Messrs. Fred Druce, Smoothy, Panter, M.V. Rees, R.A. Cooke and Mesdames Joan Bowen, Mary Dando and Jennifer Hyde. All photographs of the railway in its working days are reproduced by kind permission of Eric Rawlins.

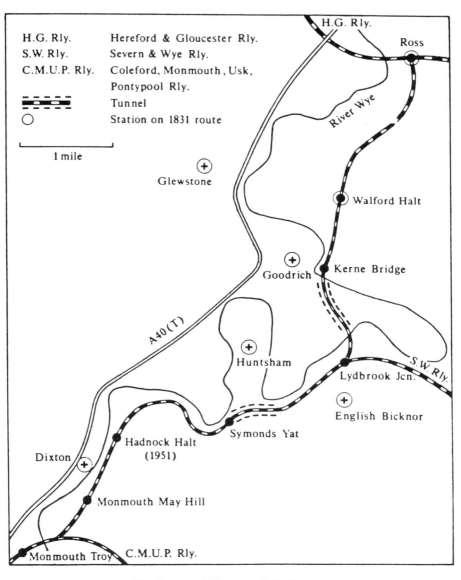

The Ross and Monmouth Railway

CHAPTER ONE

The Pre-opening Days - 1865 - 1870

On the 4th. November, 1865, four men met to discuss a new railway, a single track line running between two busy market towns on the banks of the River Wye, 12½ miles away from each other. It was not to be the first railway for either town. In 1855 the Hereford, Ross and Gloucester Railway had been opened with a station at Ross-on-Wye. At Monmouth there were three lines two of which had been horse-drawn.

After the Ross and Monmouth line had been built, only one more line was to go through Monmouth. This was the Chepstow branch of the Wye Valley Railway. The other steam drawn line was the Coleford, Monmouth, Usk and Pontypool Railway.

The 1865 attempt to build a railway was not the first as in 1831 a different rail route had been proposed but rejected.

The eventual route passed through several pretty riverside villages - Walford, Goodrich, Whitchurch, English Bicknor and Dixton - on its way from Ross to Monmouth. Ross Station was where the Great Western Railway had built it for the Hereford, Ross and Gloucester Railway. The first station was at Walford, used by people commuting to Ross and about 2½ miles from the town. 4 miles from here was Kerne Bridge Station. There is a beautiful stone bridge across the River Wye here - Kerne Bridge - and Goodrich Castle is not far away.

Lydbrook Junction was the third station and was important as it joined up with the Severn and Wye Railway (later jointly owned by the Great Western Railway and the Midland Railway) and it was originally, officially, known as the Severn and Wye Junction Station. This station also served the large Edison Swan Cable Works at English Bicknor.

Next along the line was Symonds Yat station. This, of course, was a busy station used by tourists visiting this beauty spot with its wonderful views from Symonds Yat Rock.

The last stopping place before Monmouth was at Hadnock. There had been quarry and slaughter sidings here prior to it being opened as a passenger halt in 1951.

The first of the two Monmouth stations was May Hill. This had been built as a temporary station but became permanent. Finally there was Monmouth Troy. Like May Hill it was quite a way out of Monmouth town but that was where the two other Monmouth lines terminated as well as the Ross branch. Prior to the building of the Railway a stage coach service had existed and this, in fact, continued to operate when the Railway was built, picking up passengers from the station.

The Directors of the new Railway were to be Lieutenant Colonel John Francis Vaughan, Colonel Henry Morgan Clifford, John Partridge Esq. and H.R. Luckes Esq. Colonel Vaughan was elected Chairman and he came from a

Roman Catholic family living in Courtfield on Coppet Hill near the proposed Railway. His most important ancestor was Cardinal Vaughan who founded the Mill Hill Fathers who now own Courtfield.

At the Directors' first meeting it was reported that £5,320 worth of shares had been pledged in the Monmouth area and £16,860 worth in the Ross area - £10,000 from a Mr. Beale. At their next meeting on the 9th. December 1865 it was decided that it would be desirable for the Company to oppose a Bill in Parliament for a Northampton and Banbury Junction Railway but to support a proposed Ross and Tewkesbury line. Their argument was that the Tewkesbury line would carry through traffic in conjunction with the Monmouth line providing a line between South Wales, Northamptonshire and Staffordshire whilst the Northampton line would not. However at the next meeting it was reported that the Ross and Tewkesbury proposals had been rejected but the Northampton and Banbury Line Bill was proceeding through Parliament.

The first Annual General Meeting of the Shareholders was held in 1866 and by then there were many shareholders. Two solicitors were appointed as Agents or Proxies and sold shares direct to the public. £30,400 was raised in this way. When the Directors next met it was suggested that the Railway should deviate into the Forest of Dean via Lydbrook. This would require a new station for Goodrich near Kerne Bridge and a further £20,000.

The generous Mr. Beale who had given in excess of his original £10,000 was approached for further capital for the Railway but, not surprisingly, he declined. Landowners were approached and in fact many approved, taking out shares, although the deviation to Goodrich was never made. The Firm chosen to build the Railway was led by a Mr. Firbanks who was described in the Minutes as a 'responsible, respectable Contractor'.

So the Railway started to evolve despite problems which included land ownership. In fact, because of land ownership problems near Monmouth the contractors had to start at the Ross end of the line. They began with the deep cutting at Ashfield and the erection of fencing.

There were fears that the proposed Severn and Wye Railway would upset the route of the Ross and Monmouth line and a meeting was held in London to discuss this. At this meeting the Severn and Wye Railway Company Ltd. informed the Ross and Monmouth Company that they wanted a junction with the Ross and Monmouth line at Stowfield (Lydbrook Junction) and the Company made a point of having mutual good feeling expressed in the Minutes.

There were many worries to be faced. A plan to alter the turnpike road at Kerne Bridge was explained to the Company and land ownership problems were feared. There was also a complaint from a land owner who claimed that the bridge across his occupation road was too narrow, but this was disregarded as exactly the right amount of land had been used.

As its strata seemed favourable, work on the Coppet Hill tunnel was started and soon it had visitors in the form of the Woolhope Naturalists Field Club. Whilst on a trip down the Wye they stopped near the tunnel and walked to it to investigate the ferns and fungi in it. Their Minutes reported that, after quite a long wait, a navvy appeared, lit candles and escorted the party into the tunnel. It was too dangerous to stay very long so they only had a quick look before continuing on down the River. (Woolhope Naturalists Club Transactions 1870, p.38).

By now there was enough money to complete the Railway from Ross through Walford to Kerne Bridge but money was still needed to complete the line to Monmouth. Also, having lost the battle of the gauges, the G.W.R. lines were being converted from broad gauge to standard gauge. The Hereford, Ross and Gloucester line was the first to be converted and this enabled connection with the standard gauge Monmouth line.

In August 1869 an Engineer's report was read at one of the bi-annual Shareholders meetings where it was reported that 2 miles of the line at the Monmouth end were ready for track and at the Ross end the cuttings and embankments had been excavated, bridges were in a 'forward state', the Coppet Hill tunnel was progressing well and the Severn and Wye Railway had the Company's blessing.

The next Engineer's report stated that Kerne Bridge Station had been started and only 50 yards heading was remaining. Symonds Yat tunnel had been started, 3¼ miles of permanent way had been laid and the bridges were nearly ready for use.

Kerne Bridge - relaying the points

Kerne Bridge from tunnel side

Kerne Bridge - tunnel entrance few yards beyond end of bridge

CHAPTER TWO

The Opening of the Railway

Progress was not trouble free. Mr. Firbanks, the Engineer, and his company would accept payment only in cash and not in shares. He was sent a letter about this matter and he translated this as a proposal for him to give up the Contract, so he wrote to the Company saying that he had considered their propositions to give up the Contract but recalled the terms of their Agreement which had stated that after Kerne Bridge, if work stopped for 3 years he would still have to be offered first refusal on the same terms as the original contract. The Board replied to inform Mr. Firbanks that they had no wish to terminate the Contract but they were enquiring to see how funds could be raised for the completion of the line and they had investigated contractors who would accept share payments. Matters settled down and Mr. Firbanks was informed that the line was to terminate at a junction of the Coleford Tramway at Monmouth which, it was hoped, would be taken over by the G.W.R.

By August 1870, except for the junction with the G.W.R. at Ross and the signals at Kerne Bridge, the line between these two places was ready for traction. Symonds Yat Tunnel was one quarter complete and Coppet Hill Tunnel was about to be made full size.

There was an on-going financial problem although a 'gentleman in London' was prepared to find enough money to complete the line. The Company's capital continued to shrink and Mr. Firbanks still refused to accept payment in shares. In 1871 it was proposed that the Great Western Railway Company would work the line for 60% of the profit at £26/mile/week.

A Mr. Barkley for the G.W.R. was in charge of the transaction and the Ross and Monmouth Railway Company was in favour of the proposal so an outline Agreement was drawn up for:-

"1.
The Ross and Monmouth Railway Company to enter into a new contract with Mr. Firbanks for the completion of the Ross and Monmouth Railway (to the junction with the G.W.R. extension near the Coleford turnpike road) for 10% below prices set forth in the schedule attached to Mr. Firbanks present contract, payment to be in cash monthly.
2.
The Ross and Monmouth Railway to pay Mr. Firbanks in respect of the portion of work executed and measured up to 1st. June 1870, (in addition to amounts already paid for the same) the sum of £5585 on Mr. Firbanks surrending to the Company £3,182 in 5% debentures* for undertaking to give debentures and £4,806 in ordinary shares of the Company. Mr. Firbanks to surrender all claims for interest on debentures under his present contract up to 31st. March and to complete the line in 15 months.

*Debenture Shares: Shares which do not pay dividend but fixed interest. They are rather like loans.

3.

The Ross and Monmouth Railway Company to obtain Parliamentary powers to attach Preferential Dividend of 6% to £80,000 of their present share capital.

4.

The Ross and Monmouth Railway Company to enter into a working agreement with the Great Western Railway in perpetuity subject to the Board of Trade's revision under which the Great Western Railway will find the rolling stock and will work, keep, repair and renew when necessary from time to time for the Ross and Monmouth Railway, the Great Western Railway Company guaranteeing that in no half-year shall the net payment under the said agreement be to the Ross and Monmouth Railway and to construct Monmouth Station at their own cost near that position. The Ross Station of the G.W.R. to be used for working the Ross and Monmouth Railway.

5.

The Ross and Monmouth Railway Company to abandon the portion of the line between 12 miles 40 chains on their contract plan and the contemplated junctions with the Great Western Railway.

6.

The Great Western Railway Company to approve before the signature on the working agreement, all detailed plans (including stations, bridges, permanent ways, sidings, signals etc.) of the Ross and Monmouth Railway and any modification made in these by the Great Western Railway to be subject to Mr. Barkley's sanction and approval before being agreed to by the Ross and Monmouth Railway.

7.

Mr. Barkley:-

a. to find from time to time, all money necessary to complete the line under Mr. Firbanks' original contract and plans, as modified by the G.W.R. and agreed to by him.

b. to pay Mr. Firbanks the £5,585 (see 2) at a time to be fixed.

c. to purchase all necessary land and materials needed to complete the line.

d. to pay the Ross & Monmouth Railway Company, from time to time, the sum of £7,500 in consideration of the Company using this to pay all legal and Parliamentary charges of Engineering, office expenses and secretarial charges, in cash, up to the time of the G.W.R. entering into possession of the line.

e. to pay any balance (under the conditions of Mr. Firbanks' new contract) due for work done under Mr. Firbanks' old contract since 1st. July 1870 to the present time.

f. to satisfy rent charges payable to the Company under existing agreements and the interest in debentures up to the time when the working agreement with the G.W.R. comes into force.

8.

That in consideration of forgoing these, engage in addition to other stipulations which were in force contained to hand to Mr. Barkley from time to time as work proceeds:

£80,000 into 6% preference shares

£323,200 in ordinary shares of the Company

£40,722 in the Company's debentures (bearing interest at 4%)

and also on the payment of the £5,585 to Mr. Firbanks he is to hand over to Mr. Barkley the £4,800 ordinary shares as well as the £3,182 5% debentures.

9.

Debentures corresponding to the rent charge agreed to be paid to the Duke of Beaufort, will be handed to Mr. Barkley on Mr. Barkley's arranging with the Duke for the land required under the altered conditions of the junction with the G.W.R.

10.

In the event of Mr. Barkley, at any time during the currency of this agreement, electing to deposit with the Company any sum(s) in cash, the Company shall have handed to him 6% preference shares at £20 each equivalent to the cash deposited.

11.

It is understood that the whole of the works are to be carried out under the control of the Ross & Monmouth Railway Company's Engineer and Mr. Barkley to their satisfaction.

The G.W.R. is to construct, at its own cost, the Monmouth junction and give use of Ross Station and sidings from Ross to Kerne Bridge constructed by the Ross & Monmouth Railway Company.

The present rails to be sold and the proceeds to be given to Mr. Barkley. It is understood that in the event of this agreement being carried out, the £1,200 paid on the 2nd. February and (intent therein) Mr. Firbanks is to form part of the sum to be provided by Mr. Barkley for Works."

This agreement was read, along with the working agreement, to the Directors who thought that they would be acceptable to the shareholders so they affixed their seals and hoped that the line would be complete in mid-1872.

However, delays won the day. Iron for the line from Symonds Yat to Monmouth was delayed and halted progress. In July 1872 it was said that although the line should have been ready it would not be until at least the autumn due to the state of the iron trade which was preventing the delivery of iron for a river bridge.

In January 1873 the line was still unopened, now due to the weather - but, at last, on August 1st. 1873, Colonel Rich - the Chief Engineer of the G.W.R. - came to inspect the line. The inspecting party walked along the line, through tunnels, over bridges, peering and prodding everything they saw. Several times the 'Gallant Colonel' as the Ross Gazette described him, ordered the maximum weight that the bridges would ever have to carry should be taken onto the bridges.

After several suggestions had been made, Colonel Rich expressed satisfaction and gave permission for the line to be opened.

Large posters and timetables appeared all around the place and the preparations were made. But - later that night Colonel Rich said that the line could not open as planned! He had discovered that there was not a turn-table at Monmouth so the light tender engine could not turn - so one way it would be dangerous as the tender - running first - would obstruct the driver's view. For two days disappointment reigned at yet another delay and each day large numbers of would-be passengers arrived at the station only to be told the train would not run as planned.

On the third day however, the problem was solved. It was described in the Ross Gazette like this:-

"No time, however, was lost and after several communications had passed between the managers and Colonel Rich, permission was given to use what is called a tank engine which dispenses with the necessity of a tender".

So, at last, on Monday 3rd. August the Town Crier was sent round confirming the opening of the line on that day. Seven minutes later than timed a tank engine, hauling eight full carriages, steamed out of Ross Station with very little ceremony.

"If it was tame", the Ross Gazette explained, "It was soon shown that there was business meant and the officials at the stations along the route were civil, prompt and energetic".

Their reporter described a comfortable ride through some of the most beautiful scenery in the country which he, said, "no pen can truly describe". He said that not many Monmouth people believed that the railway was at last open so there was not much of a welcome nor were there many people on the return journey.

But - at last - the Ross & Monmouth Railway was open!

Ross-on-Wye Station

CHAPTER THREE

The Course of the Railway

ROSS

Ross Station had quite a complicated branch layout with two signal-boxes, a turntable and various other buildings.

As the Station was approached from the north, a line left the main line to go to the Goods Shed and five other sidings. The Goods Depot was opposite the north signal-box which was replaced in 1915 and closed in 1938.

The track then forked out to curve round the passenger platforms. On the west side of the platforms a line led down towards the Engine Shed and turntable and the line to Monmouth. The east track led to the Hereford, Ross & Gloucester Line and the south signal-box that was closed in 1938 but which was replaced by a new signal-box replacing both the south and north boxes. The turn-table which had been used solely for turning the locomotive around had a siding added in 1920 and by this time a loading dock and cattle pens had also been added providing the livestock accommodation so necessary in such an agriculturally intensive area as Ross. The Engine Shed was closed in October 1963.

Ross-on-Wye signal box

WALFORD

Walford was a very simple little halt, serving the dormitory village of Walford. It was opened in 1931 and only had one platform.

KERNE BRIDGE

Kerne Bridge Station was slightly larger than Walford. It had two platforms and originally, sidings. One of these held an old G.W.R. dormitory coach which remained until a few years ago. The line divided into two providing a passing loop but this loop was broken in 1901 when a section of track was removed. All the points were operated by two ground frames. The station building still exists and has recently been repaired and used as youth accommodation.

Kerne Bridge Station now used as small residential accommodation unit

Kerne Bridge Station
New extension at far end is small dormitory

10

LYDBROOK JUNCTION

Lydbrook Junction Station was one of the largest stations on the Railway and served the Edison Swan Cable Works. It had three main platform islands and three-signal boxes. The two older signal-boxes were taken out of use at an unknown date and the third was added before 1925 and closed on 26th. February 1961. The main sidings were removed in 1949. As the station was approached from Kerne Bridge, the Edison Swan Works were on the left. There were two single platforms, the left-hand one serving the Severn and Wye Railway which closed on January 30th. 1956. A peculiarly shaped platform - similar to a filled in 'A' was between these two single platforms.

Coppet Tunnel - Lydbrook End

Lydbrook Junction viaduct

SYMONDS YAT

Symonds Yat was another simple station with two platforms and a passing loop. The section of track that made up the passing loop was taken out of use in 1953, as was the signal-box. The Waiting Room stood in a rather risky position overhanging the River Wye, supported by two iron girders. Waiting travellers could look out over the white waters of the Wye Rapids!

HIGH MEADOW, HADNOCK QUARRY & HADNOCK HALT

There were a series of halts and sidings just before Monmouth. The Slaughter siding was a Forestry Commission siding built under an agreement of May 1870. At High Meadow a further timber siding was built under an agreement of July 1920. At Hadnock itself there was a halt and quarry which belonged to the Robert and Lewis Company.

MONMOUTH (MAY HILL)

This station was designed as a temporary terminus for the Railway whilst the extension to Troy was being built, but it was actually kept as a station. As the station was approached from Hadnock a siding, owned by the Ministry of Food, struck off to the left - this had been added in 1942. Further on the right-hand side were the platform and signal-box and one or two other sidings, one being used by the Monmouth Coal and Iron Company.

Symonds Yat

Sleeper and fittings near Hadnock 1983

Monmouth, May Hill

MONMOUTH (TROY)

The other terminus of the Railway was a junction for three railways, the Ross and Monmouth Railway, the Coleford, Monmouth, Usk and Pontypool Railway and the Chepstow branch of the Wye Valley Railway. All three railways were to be absorbed into the G.W.R.

Because of the amount of traffic the line would have to carry this station had quite a complicated layout. As the station was approached from May Hill the marshalling sidings were on the right and the line to Chepstow was to the left. The signal-box was just before the platforms and there was a goods shed and some cattle pens in the marshalling yards. Although no details are to hand this layout changed in 1956. The line to Usk closed in 1955 and passenger services finished on the Chepstow line in 1959.

The completed line was 12½ miles long. Its steepest gradient was 1 in 100 (1%) and its sharpest curve had a radius of 14 chains (924 yards).

There were 7 bridges, one of stone and the others were cast or wrought iron girders with stone abutments and 7 had wooden tops. The remainder had iron girders.

There were 2 viaducts, one with 9 spans and the other with 8.

There were two tunnels, Coppet Hill Tunnel was 634 yards long and Symonds Yat Tunnel was 434 yards long.

There was just the one turntable - at Ross.

On the approach to Ross was the large Ashfield Cutting which had a very soft appearance due to the reddish tint of the sandstone in the Wye area.

The line travelled across a complex of cuttings, embankments and bridges in the red sandstone.

This Railway was a great memorial for the ingenuity of the Victorian engineers.

BR sign at Monmouth Troy, 1984

CHAPTER FOUR

The First 60 Years, 1873 - 1930

Now the Railway was open it settled down to a quiet life - or more or less so!

The Directors were told of a petition sent in by Symonds Yat residents for the Railway to provide goods accommodation. They were also told that the Manager of the Wye Colliery Company had requested a coal wharf at Kerne Bridge Station - this enquiry had to go to the G.W.R. Someone even requested more Monmouth trains on Race Days! Sunday trains were run against the approval of the G.W.R.

In June 1885, the G.W.R. agreed to run two extra trains on the line and the railway became busier. But the G.W.R. was still dissatisfied with the Railway itself. Stop blocks and a 5 ton crane for Kerne Bridge were requested together with a footpath and steps at Symonds Yat.

The Directors appointed a former Goods guard as the Inspector of Goods and he was paid 35/- a week (£1.75p).

On October 2nd. 1875, it was reported that 197,964½ passengers had been carried between August 4th. 1873 and June 20th. 1875 divided into classes as listed:-

10,654½ passengers (approximately 5%) had travelled 1st. Class
27,389 passengers (approximately 15%) had travelled 2nd. Class
159,921 passengers (approximately 80%) had travelled 3rd. Class.

The Directors considered this to prove the advantage of the Line.

The Goods figures were not as satisfactory. Only 38,000 tons of goods had been transported between 9th. August 1873 and 30th. June 1875. Most through traffic had been sent by other, longer, routes and this was the traffic that was considered to be important. As a result the Directors were prepared to take the G.W.R., who were responsible for this, to the Railway Commissioners. The trouble was eventually resolved without recourse to the Courts.

In 1881, Colonel John Vaughan died. He had been elected Chairman at the first meeting of Directors and after his death his son, Captain Francis Vaughan was asked to take his father's place as Chairman.

In the 1890's the Railway reached its peak with 24 passenger and 18 Goods trains arriving daily on both lines at Ross. 1892's figures were very impressive. The total income was £4,489 including rent from the G.W.R., the rent from surplus land and fees. The expenditure was £1,625 including Income Tax, Directors' fees, interest and rents, loans and the G.W.R's expenses, making a working profit of £2,864. The dividend to Shareholders for every £20 share was 12/- (60p) for Preference Shares and 2/6 (12½p) for Ordinary Shares. This paid back about £131.3s.6d (131.17½p).

Although the area was well advertised in G.W.R. booklets trade was not so buoyant by the end of 1893 and passenger profits dropped by £219. Trade was generally declining. Because of agricultural and mining depression and new dairy imports from Denmark, the whole country had a few bad years. Things were picking up in the first half of 1896 but a smallpox epidemic was mainly responsible for a fallback in the second half of the year.

Once Railway business picked up, the fares were reduced. The 1st. Class charge was twice the 3rd. Class fare and the return ticket was 1.2/3rds the price of the single fare.

In 1897 the G.W.R. requested more accommodation at May Hill, the cost of a new station being £2,794. They also wanted a siding and boarding platform for horses and cattle at Kerne Bridge. The G.W.R. was getting more adventurous as two years earlier they had put in a claim to buy Ashburton Road in Ross although this was withdrawn. The two Companies were constantly fighting to keep their expenditure low.

In 1903 a move was made to expand the Ross Urban District Council's area and as this would have led to higher rates the G.W.R. allowed the Ross and Monmouth Company 10/- (50p) to fight the case.

In 1905, the G.W.R. bought the Wye Valley line and the Ross and Monmouth Company feared this would mean them losing £17 per month. Their fears were justified as they started losing trade in the region of £200 per annum.

By 1909 trade was progressing well. Income was £4,845 and expenditure was £1,899 giving a working profit of £2,946. The Directors' fees were lower than in 1893 and whilst the dividend on Preference Shares was the same as then, the dividend on Ordinary Shares rose by one shilling (5p) to 3/6 (17½p) for £20 shares.

In February 1911 the Ross Traders Association requested an improved service on the Line and this was achieved by July 10th. By 1913 the accounts for the first half of the year showed a working profit of £3,817. This included £1,902 passenger income, £2,186 for Goods working, £425 for parcels and £50 for mail.

A great deal of Army traffic was carried between 1914-18 and this disrupted the routine. However 1916 was a good year for the Railway and the profit was up to £5,390. The dividends paid out remained unchanged and this was still the case in 1919 when the profits were £4,428.

Income and Expenditure was entered in the Minutes for last time in 1922 when the income had been £9,931 and the expenditure £5,569 leaving a working profit of £4,362.

TABLE TO SHOW THE RAILWAY'S INCOME 1895 - 1910

YEAR	TOTAL INCOME	Passenger 1st half year	2nd half year	Freight 1st half year	2nd half year
1895	8023	+	+	-	-
1896	8042	+	-	+	-
1897	7898	-	+	-	+
1898	7985	-	+	-	+
1899	8265	+	+	+	+
1900	8534	+	+	+	-
1901	8728	-	-	-	+
1902	8979	+	+	+	-
1903	9074	+	-	+	+
1904	9408	+	+	+	+
1905	8759	-	-	-	-
1906	8963	+	+	-	+
1907	8852	-	-	+	+
1908	8855	-	+	+	-
1909	8573	+	-	-	-
1910	8809	-	-	+	+

+ increase on previous half year   - decrease on previous half year

Here the Company's Minutes ended and the Great Western Railway took over under their preliminary absorption scheme of the 1921 Railways Act.

For a long while the Line was used for a through service from Pontypool Road, through Monmouth and on to Ross. The Chepstow branch ran separately with about five services a day. A connection was made between the branches three times a day which made busy times for all the stations.

From the 1880's onwards the Summer Holiday excursions run by the G.W.R. were very popular. For 5/- (25p) 1st. Class, 3/6 (17½p) 2nd. Class and 2/6 (12½p) 3rd. Class it was possible to travel from Ross to Tintern. This train also connected with others at Bristol, Bath, Cheltenham, Gloucester, Stroud, Newport, Cardiff and Hereford as well as many smaller stations.

It is also interesting to note that in 1903, Ross Golf Club was founded and on two or three tee shots it was necessary to cross the railway line!

The fares, in the early part of the century, from Ross to Kerne Bridge were about 4d (2p) but because of the value of money at that time many people walked 3 or 4 miles out of their way to catch the ferry for only 1d!

For a long time rail was the safest and most comfortable way to travel but in 1929 the Ross Gazette reported that "stones, believed to have been placed by children, on the Ross - Monmouth railway line between Symonds Yat and Lydbrook caused the derailment of a gangers' motor trolley. One of the two men on the trolley suffered a fractured ankle, lacerated scalp and slight concussion" and in 1930 "following the crash of a boulder weighing several tons from the cliffs at Symonds Yat onto the railway line, causing a derailment of a passenger train, an examination of the cliffs disclosed that there were thousands of tons of rock which had become loosened and which presented a real danger - the **G.W.R.** was taking remedial action".

Ross-on-Wye

Engine Shed - Ross-on-Wye now Architectural Antiques Business
Note original size of arch for wide gauge

CHAPTER FIVE

The Railway at Work - 1928 - 1960

During the early part of this period we can paint a nostalgic, story-book picture of the Railway. Sunday Schoolchildren would be transported to their annual 'bun-fight' near Goodrich, tourists would enjoy the spectacular ride alongside the beautiful River Wye, cows, horses and, sometimes, pigeons would be transported as well as the ordinary passengers going about their daily lives. The stations were kept tidy in the true Great Western tradition, Station Masters wore neat black caps and the brass buttons on their uniforms were kept well polished. The seats on the station had 'G.W.R.' proudly emblazoned on them as did the carriages and engines. The little push-pull autocars went, fussily, about their business and the freight trains shunted to and fro. The signalmen seemed snug in their warm signal-boxes and everybody went about their jobs quietly and efficiently. Ross and Monmouth (Troy) were both busy stations because they were junctions of railways running through attractive countryside. A replacement serviced engine came to Ross from Hereford every ten days or so and the previous one went back.

However, the Wye rises quickly and at times the line would be flooded. When this happened the trains had to slow to nearly walking pace and the fireman had to watch that the fire was not extinguished. The problem was that part of the Railway had been built on the Wye flood plains and the floods would 'swallow' up the rails and sometimes the platforms, especially at Kerne Bridge, so that then services had to stop altogether.

The train, nicknamed the Monmouth Bullet because of its lack of speed ran quite a busy timetable. The train also had another nickname - the Coffee Pot - because during gaps in the timetable, the train would stand by the platform 'hissing like a polished kettle on a warm hob!

The following timetables were from the year 1938:-

SUNDAYS

STATION	a.m.	p.m.	STATION	a.m.	
Ross-on-Wye	10.10	7.15	Monmouth Troy	2.36	6.00
Kerne Bridge	10.19	7.25	Monmouth May Hill	2.39	6.03
Lydbrook Jct.	10.24	7.29	Symonds Yat	2.49	6.13
Symonds Yat	10.29	7.34	Lydbrook Jct.	2.54	6.18
Monmouth May Hill	10.40	7.45	Kerne Bridge	2.58	6.22
Monmouth Troy	10.43	7.30	Ross-on-Wye	3.08	6.32

STATION	a.m.	a.m.	a.m.	a.m.	p.m.	p.m.	p.m.	p.m.	p.m.	p.m.
Ross-on-Wye	6.40	7.13	8.22	10.57	11.46	1.50	3.01	4.30	5.10	7.25
Kerne Bridge	6.50	7.23	8.32	11.07	11.56	2.00	3.11	4.40	5.20	7.35
Lydbrook Jct.	6.54	7.26	8.36	11.11	11.59	2.04	3.15	4.44	5.24	7.39
Symonds Yat	6.59	-	8.41	11.16	-	2.08	3.20	-	5.29	7.44
M'm'th M.Hill	7.08	-	8.50	11.25	-	-	3.30	-	5.38	7.53
Monmouth Troy	7.14	-	8.55	11.28	-	-	3.37	-	5.42	7.58
				p.m.	p.m.	p.m.	p.m.	p.m.	p.m.	p.m
Monmouth Troy	7.24	-	9.46	-	12.40	-	3.51	-	6.20	8.43
M'm'th M Hill	727	-	9.50	-	12.44	-	3.54	-	6.24	8.47
Symonds Yat	7.37	-	10.00	-	12.54	2.20	4.04	-	6.34	8.57
Lydbrook Jct.	7.42	8.00	10.07	12.10	12.59	2.24	4.09	4.50	6.39	9.02
Kerne Bridge	7.46	8.04	10.11	12.14	1.03	2.29	4.13	4.54	6.43	9.06
Monmouth Troy	7.53	8.13	10.20	12.23	1.12	2.38	4.22	5.03	6.52	9.17

Early in 1931 Ross Urban Council investigated the possibilities of advertising the town as a tourist resort. They followed this through and this, along with the G.W.R. tourist season ticket facilities, added to the Line's tourist traffic. The costs for one week's travel was:-

15/9 (approx. 76p) for 1st Class and 10/6 (approx. 52½p) for 3rd. Class.

G.W.R. timetables in the mid-1930's encouraged day trippers from South Wales, Bristol and the Midlands to visit the spectacular scenery of this exceptionally beautiful area. The people of Herefordshire and the Forest of Dean added to the character of the Line, particularly in the Symonds Yat area, by opening Tea Rooms and Boarding Houses. At Ross a Refreshments Room was run by a Miss Alsop. She made a point of arriving early and providing a cup of tea for the staff before business started.

A Goods Guard worked from 8.30 a.m. - 4.30 p.m. The stock that used to run the Railway was typical of a small branch railway. 0-6-2 T's were very common as were 0-4-2 T's. Nothing heavier than a 2-6-2 T could be carried on the Line anyway. At times the occasional G.W.R. railcar would be used to convey the passengers. Open door carriages were often used behind the locomotive and usually trains consisted of one or two coaches although sometimes longer trains were necessary. There were two engines - one pulling passengers and one freight and if a spare was needed it had to be brought from Hereford. The only Ground Frame was at Symonds Yat.

Mr. Mike Rees worked the line in the 1950's based in the Signal and Telegraph Workshop which was situated between the Ross/Gloucester platforms. His work covered the maintenance of telephones and signal-boxes between Monmouth and Ross. He recalls colleagues who would 'blow the whistle' as they passed through to Tudorville as a greeting to their Mums! He also recalls that it was satisfying for boys travelling to school at Monmouth to throw the girls' shoes out of the windows when the occasion was right. Mr. Rees has continued his railway interests as Curator of the Great Western

Railway Museum at Coleford, which is housed in one of the last remaining permanent railway buildings in the Forest of Dean on the original site of Coleford Railway Yard. Amongst his 'visual aids' is a video 'Railway Round-about' produced by W.H. Smith which features - if not strictly accurately - scenes from the Ross and Monmouth railway in action.

Part of dismantled line at Tudorville.
The footpath is named after one of Ross' twin towns

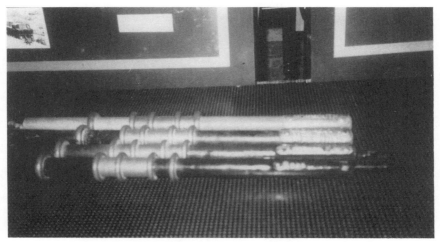

Staffs used on Ross & Monmouth Railway now on display in
GWR Museum, Coleford

21

Many, now more mature citizens, remember running alongside the 'Bullet' and standing on the bridges as it travelled below. The Railway had its busy times but when the 'Coffee Pot' was at rest all was quiet at Ross Station and it was perfectly possible to walk around the deserted station without a platform ticket.

The Stationmaster's house at Symonds Yat was the red-brick house which stands on the hill past the Saracens Head and the only way up to this was by a flight of steps. There was still a pump in the yard in 1928! The signalman at Symonds Yat lived at the other end of the tunnel and had to walk through it to work. The tunnel was also used as footpath by others. Ernest Viles was Stationmaster from 1921-28 and his daughter Mary (now Dando) recalls how, as a little girl, her mother would walk with her through the tunnel so that she could play with the signalman's daughter. Mrs. Dando also recalls being given rides on the Gangers' trolley! Between the ages of 5 and 8 Mrs. Dando travelled to school by train to Monmouth in the care of the guard as this was easier than being walked to school at Whitchurch.

Mrs. Dando also remembers crates of pigeons being brought by train, off-loaded and then released to find their way home. Well-to-do people would travel 1st. Class in order to fish for salmon and, of course, would stay at the Royal Hotel which stands by the station entrance. Many trippers would arrive from Birmingham for trips on the river - by rowing boat of course. School-children were transported from all stations from Ross to Monmouth and Mrs. Joan Bowen remembers walking daily through the fields by the river from Huntsham (now the Open Farm) to Symonds Yat to catch the train. She also remembers the gypsies who regularly camped in the fields along the way and these caused her some trepidation as she walked by. Symonds Yat Station frequently won the Station Gardens Competitions. Mrs. Jennifer Hyde remembers that in the 1950's her sister used to pay 8d (4p) half-return from Lydbrook Junction to Symonds Yat where she worked at the Royal Hotel.

In 1948 the Great Western Railway was absorbed into British Railways and life was somewhat changed. Some workers resigned and those remaining changed their uniforms. Instead of G.W.R's mixed locomotives most of the workload was carried by B.R's standard tank engines and closed carriages. Freight traffic did not change much e.g. cable was still carried from Lydbrook Junction.

The Line was not now as important as it had been and most people knew that unless there was big investment the railways throughout England would be hitting hard times. Rolling stock and stations throughout the country had suffered badly during the Second World War and rapid rebuilding was impossible. The railway became a very bad competitor to the roads as petrol was becoming cheaper and road travel more convenient. Locally, people were moving from the area to work in Gloucester and the Midlands and many of those who remained in the area used cars for convenience. New road building increased the drift from the railways particularly when the Ross Spur was developed and a fast dual carriageway linked Ross and Monmouth. Holiday patterns were changing and visitors came to the area by coach rather than by train. By the late 1950's going abroad was both easier and cheaper and this led to fewer visitors coming to the Wye Valley.

Freight traffic was affected by the decline in production from the uneconomic pits of the Forest of Dean. Lorry transport could cope more easily and directly with heavy local loads and parcel traffic was developed both by local buses and the centralised National Carriers services based in Gloucester.

At last, with the fall in passenger traffic, closure was imminent and on the 5th. January 1959 the last passenger train was run from Monmouth to Ross. It was played out by Ross Town Band playing Auld Lang Syne. It left Monmouth to the loud explosions of fog detonators and the locomotive's shrill whistle. It rattled through the snow covered valley, whistling continuously. As it hurtled past the little stations, figures huddled together giving their farewells to the familiar coaches and tank engine. On that day too, the last train was to travel from Monmouth to Chepstow leaving the town of Monmouth without a railway.

When the last train ran on the Ross and Monmouth line, B.R. put a souvenir ticket office in it. The Ross Gazette reported that the tickets, with the Great Western Railway, printed on them were very popular and that this brought £35 back to B.R. What was more fantastic was that 125 tickets were sold at Monmouth Station as it was very common for no tickets at all to be sold there. The train steamed into Ross for the last time but the Railway continued to carry goods and a B.R. spokesman said that work on improving the signalling for freight was to commence immediately.

The day after the official closure the Midland branch of the Stephenson Locomotive Society chartered a train to carry them from Chepstow - Ross - Chepstow and more than 400 avid enthusiasts clambered onto the 8 carriage train. The Ross Gazette said of them, 'On the train young men pored over timetables, charts and other railway literature and logged the time the train passed each station and halt! It was hardly the exit the Railway deserved.

Following re-examination of branch lines by the British Railways Board under Dr. Beeching, the only stretch remaining between Ross and Lydbrook was closed, on 1st. November 1965. The last train consisted of 5 brake vans hauled by a B.R. Class 2 standard tank engine. In the brake vans were ten enthusiasts who were making a circular journey from Gloucester, through Ross to Lydbrook Junction and back to Gloucester via Ross. A faint cheer was raised as the train shunted out for the last time. How would the Directors of that Railway have felt seeing the line close 100 years after the first real attempt and 134 years after the first idea to open it. What would Colonel Vaughan have thought of our modern locomotives and rolling stock?

The line had had a good life but would it be viable today? Could a Preservation Society have bought it and run it successfully? None of these questions can really be answered but it is true that the railway had made its mark on the Wye Valley.

Viaduct at Monmouth

Post and rail fencing near Ross

CHAPTER SIX

The Last Remains

Several features remained after the Railway was dismantled. Street names like Station Street and Station Approach still live on and business like the Coalyards which would have been supplied by rail still exist. The old station site at Ross is now the Ashburton Industrial Estate and some of the old station buildings house small businesses. Up, on a rise, stands the old engine shed that was used for both the Ross and Monmouth Railway and the Hereford to Gloucester Line. It now serves as a showroom for a thriving firm selling architectural antiques. It is interesting to note that the doorway was changed from the original - this happened when the gauge was changed.

The magnificent curve that took the Railway out of Ross is still obvious, next to the 'bus depot. It is possible to get back onto the line on the other side of Gloucester Road. Here cuttings and embankments kept the Line as level as possible and recently the area has been cleared to make walking easier as this is a favourite walk for locals. A little further on is the Ashfield Cutting. The bridge is still intact although the area underneath has been filled in. An attractive childrens play area has been developed here in memory of a former Councillor. Some of the original post and rail fencing remains.

The track then crossed over into Tudorville where a modern housing estate has now been developed. In May 1991 part of the old track-bed was named Betzdorf Walk after one of Ross' two twin towns. This half mile stretch has been turned into a grassy footpath with picnic benches and was inaugurated during a visit of a party of Germans from Betzdorf.

Further on, at Walford, there is now a building on the level station site. Between Walford and Kerne Bridge (SO 585206 - 582192) the line is marked by an avenue of poplar trees. Here again bridges and fencing are intact. At Kerne Bridge Station the station building remains and until recently retained the old G.W.R. character. However, recent renovations have taken away some of this and also the old railway camping coach which was used as a dormitory for the Adventure Centre which uses the site.

The entrance to Coppet Hill Tunnel can be reached by following the line of the track and it is possible to walk through it. There is a bend after a short distance and up to this point it is very dark as the 'light at the end of the tunnel' comes once the bend is rounded. A torch and sturdy boots are necessary for this adventure! At the Welsh Bicknor entrance (SO 588178) the portal is partly bricked up but is, nevertheless, impressive. A lineside call-box is still recognisable here. This tunnel is a remarkable feature hewn out of Coppet Hill's quartz conglomerate.

Almost immediately after the line emerged from the tunnel it crossed the river by an iron girder bridge - care is needed where some of the wooden planks have rotted. Not only does the track-bed remain but also a footpath runs alongside to what was the Edison Swan's Cable Works. There is a packaging factory on the site now.

25

Between SO 586176 and 565159 the line can be followed, by the Wye. Some G.W.R. boundary markers remain, now decayed and rusty.

The portals for Symonds Yat Tunnel remain although it is not possible to walk through it - indeed the nearby Hotel has built a high bank to the rear of their car park, almost across the mouth of the tunnel!

The station site at Symonds Yat is now the car park for the Royal Hotel and the layout is still visible although none of the buildings remain. It is still possible to see the steel struts that once held the precariously balanced Waiting Room that hung over the river (see Chapter Five).

Between Hadnock and May Hill the track can be walked along by the river and is part of the Wye Valley Walk. Recently parts of the path have been cleared and in one place, near to the Biblins Bridge, a stone culvert has been revealed showing attention to detail not always evident in today's constructions.

Remains of the station buildings still exist at Hadnock Quarry and between Little Hadnock and Hadnock siding platform mounds are just visible.

Between Hadnock and May Hill the track can be walked along, by the river, for quite some way until May Hill itself where the station site is now being used as a light industrial estate.

There is a marvellous river bridge connecting the two Monmouth stations together. This extension was opened on 1st. May 1874.

The station buildings at Troy remain in very good condition for their age. The track-bed is rather weeded over but signal-posts still remain. The station was of a very typical G.W.R. design with the usual Great Western frills. This is now also used for light industry.

Not only stations remain; small lineside units by the Wye are used as fishing huts. Sleepers can be found if you look carefully and have been used for many different purposes such as fencing and boundary markers. Slag used as ballast is evident and track-beds are well walked footpaths. The Wye Valley walk follows parts of the line crossing the Railway at Ross and picking up again at Welsh Bicknor.

It then follows the route of the Railway for most of the way to Wyesham, Monmouth Mayhill and Monmouth Troy. Details of this Walk are obtainable from Tourist Offices in the area.

Many lost their jobs when Beeching's axe fell and many still love the romance of steam and would not be happy with today's trains. Many other branch lines suffered the same fate as the Ross and Monmouth and these railways which, for over a century, were an essential part of the British landscape have left little behind them but their memories.

Symonds Yat - line of railway now part of the Wye Valley Walk

Symonds Yat from trackbed

CHAPTER SEVEN

The Future?

During the past few years plans have been underway to re-instate the railway in the Wye Valley and the route of the Ross and Monmouth Railway is included in the scheme. Mr. Eric Rawlins, a retired railwayman and enthusiast of rail travel, is dedicating his life to the project. His aim is to turn a dream into reality before the turn of the century and the proposal is for a railway to run again from Hereford and Ross to Gloucester and from Chepstow to Monmouth and Ross, linking with existing main lines to provide nationwide and international - through the Tunnel - links.

Similar obstacles confront the Board of the Wye Valley Railway to-day as confronted the Directors of the Ross and Monmouth Railway in the 1860's. Farmers and other 'interested parties' turned a Public Meeting, outlining the proposals, into a vicious haranguing match. Those who spoke for the railways were swamped by those who could see no value in any kind of reconstruction, or felt they had something to lose. As in the 1860's, doubts were expressed about the motives of the anti-railway lobby and the resulting atmosphere was not pleasant.

However, the scheme is still alive and Mr. Rawlins mounts a display at the annual Carnival and other events. International consultants, Cass Hayward, produced a feasibility study and detailed financial estimates put the reconstruction costs at £37 million. The Directors of the Company have also ordered a cost-benefit analysis of the project and local interests, on both sides, remain active. A Market Research Company was commissioned to carry out a survey of potential customers in the Summer of 1993 and a questionnaire was distributed to all householders in the areas around the routes as well as being widely available. Initial indications showed a positive response to the project.

The proposed railway would be standard gauge with electric motive power. In the Draft Financial Projection of 1987 it was stated that 'during the process of re-instatement it is suggested that motive power is provided by diesel rail-car units complete, although it may be possible to install the necessary equipment (posts and catenary etc.) as re-instatement proceeds'. The WVR is determined that the line be built to British Rail standards so that main line diversions may be accommodated. The determination of the Company to create an electrified line is a point of great interest. On the environmental side there is considerable opposition to the erection of overhead gantries and catenary, however slim they may be, as the routes run through extremely attractive countryside and the stated aims of the WVR are to 'provide a modern, useful and environmentally unobtrusive service'. Radio signalling would be employed.

On a more practical note, the use of 25KV electrification is a brave move since evidence suggests that the neighbouring regions of British Rail will not be similarly equipped, certainly this century. The first part of the former Western region to be electrified will be the proposed overground Paddington to Heathrow line.   Towards the end of the decade it is likely that the new Crossrail link will bring wire to Reading in 1996-7.   It maybe that Network South East feels it necessary to electrify lines from Paddington to Oxford via Didcot, but expensive investment in new diesel rolling stock makes this seem unlikely.   With nowhere else for the IC 125 HST sets to be cascaded it seems unlikely that the western side of the region will be electrified in the foreseeable future, although privatisation (or a change of government) may alter this state of affairs.

It may be that the re-instatement of a small section of line along one of the more scenic parts of the route, perhaps from Monmouth to Symonds Yat, using DMU's, would attract passengers in such a way that some of the opposition might be overcome.   This is a six to seven mile stretch bordered by forest on one side and the River Wye on the other, with the basic trackbed in fairly good condition.

There are many small villages along the proposed route and the main road (A49) from Hereford to Ross in particular seems prone to serious accidents. The A466 Monmouth to Chepstow road is also attractive but tortuous.   The area abounds with tourists for most of the year and many people commute between Hereford, Gloucester, Ross and Monmouth, even as far as the Midlands, so there are, indeed, considerable attractions in the adoption of the railway solution to reduce road usage.

From photographs reproduced in this book it is obvious that the original track routes are severely overgrown and bridges are either completely non-existent or in a poor state.   A walk through the Coppet Hill tunnel is quite an experience - particularly with a group of youngsters!   (A Youth Hostel is close by the Welsh Bicknor portal).   Most of the tunnel is straight but there is a bend towards the northern end, so part of the walk is in total darkness and it is very squelchy underfoot.   Drips fall eerily from the roof landing with a loud 'splosh' on the ground but there is a sense of achievement, especially felt by the leaders of the groups, on emerging into daylight.

The proposed route indicates some 19 halts in addition to the main stations at Hereford, Ross, Monmouth, Gloucester and Chepstow, therefore a great deal of constructional work is entailed as well as the track re-instatement.

Many hurdles remain to be crossed in this ambitious scheme.   The estimated cost in 1987 was £37 million and naturally increases year by year. Legally much work is involved in order to regain all the required land, much of which has been appropriated through various means for other uses, including the Wye Valley Walk and at the Forest Hotel, Symonds Yat, a high bank has been built in front of the tunnel entrance.   At Ross a Housing Association has built a complex of homes on the site of the former cattle market and in the process has removed the high bank along which the railway ran in order to accommodate the estate.

If the railway is rebuilt further problems continue in the form of realisation of passenger and freight traffic, permanent way maintenance, motive power, signalling (albeit a particularly simple route) and running costs.

Principal highlighted features of reconstruction are:

*   track-bed clearing and re-instatement
*   bridges - repair and reconstruction
*   drainage works on parts of the line, in particular areas close to the river which in times of the Ross and Monmouth Railway were susceptible to flooding

* construction of level crossings - this leads to problems at Ross in particular where the relief road crosses the route
* reconstruction of old stations and halts, some of which are now occupied (at Tintern there are tea-rooms and a picnic site) and construction of new ones
* the appeasing or residents who bought properties in good faith and now discover they might have an EMU, or even Mallard, running along the line at the end of the garden.

The local press reports on progress from time to time and correspondents air their views through the Letters columns. The eventual outcome is awaited with interest.

CHAPTER EIGHT

Links with the Wider World

The Ross and Monmouth Railway was not only useful as a local railway. It provided links to railways radiating across the country. From Ross, the Hereford and Gloucester Railway could be used to travel to Hereford and then via the Great Western and London & North Western railways northwards to Shrewsbury, North Wales and, eventually, Scotland. By travelling eastwards to Gloucester connections could be made to Oxford, London and the South-East. From Monmouth, the Coleford, Monmouth, Usk & Pontypool Railway (CMUP) provided links to South Wales and the Chepstow link through Tintern provided access to the G.W.R. South Wales to London line.

Although all these lines ran through some beautiful countryside, passenger traffic was not the prime reason for their construction. Iron ore and coal transportation was of great importance in the middle of the 19th. century and many tramways existed to link with the railway systems. Remnants of both rail and tramways are visible in many parts of the Forest of Dean and Forest Trails leaflets - available from Forest Enterprise and Tourist Offices - give interesting insights into the intensive industrial scene of the last century. Most trails are around four miles in length but with a little imagination one can feel the busy atmosphere that once prevailed in now derelict pit heads and mine workings.

Monmouth Town was aware of the advantages the railway could bring and actively helped to promote the Ross and Monmouth Railway but, as always, legal procedures and land acquisitions etc., took years to complete and by this time industrial patterns had changed considerably. Ores from Northamptonshire and other parts of the world could be more rapidly transported via the main lines making the Forest of Dean less important. The G.W.R. absorbed many small lines and saw no need to develop more rural branch lines. This led to the decline of existing small lines. They were still important for the school-children and commuters who needed quick transportation from home to work-place and they provided pleasant excursions for town dwellers from Birmingham, Bristol and further afield. Mixed and agricultural freight was also carried and this continued for several years after passenger services had ceased. As with many rural towns, and indeed some larger towns, Monmouth's stations were not situated in the centre of the town. Both were on the opposite side of the river and Monmouth Troy was about a mile to the South-West of the town.

The Wye Valley annually attracts many thousands of visitors and during the railway era many arrived by train, providing employment for what, to us, seems a large number of personnel. In Fred Druce's book 'The Light of Other Days' a photograph of Symonds Yat Station at the turn of the century shows six railway employees. The smartness of the station and availability of staff to help holidaymakers with luggage was considered to be very important in a holiday centre. In Chapter Five it is recalled that this station frequently won the Best Kept Station Award and even today stations compete for this accolade. Towards the end of the railway era it would appear that less people were employed as Fred Druce describes the 'porter - cum ticket-collector-cum station-master' announcing the arrival of a train at Ross from Gloucester.

The opening of the line was greeted with much shouting and flag-waving. There were speeches and the engines had Union flags flying on them. After the first train from Hereford to Gloucester had passed through Ross a party was held at the Goods station for a large number of children. There was a public Tea at the Market House and later on Balls were held there and at the Royal Hotel (Ross). A local railway Director provided a dinner for the railway navvies at what is now the Conservative Club and the evening ended with a Fireworks Display.

As at Monmouth, Ross people had to walk to the outskirts of their town to catch a train and also had to walk along dark, muddy lanes. It would appear that 'filthy and disgusting paths' are not just a vagary of present times and people would write as irately to their local paper then as now! Perhaps these public pressures led to street improvements as effectively then as public outcry does today; the dirty alley became Cantilupe Road.

If you travel on the Severn Valley Railway today you will pass through Ross Station at Kidderminster - well, almost, as the station was modelled on Ross-on-Wye. There is reference to this in the Railway Magazine of April 1987 (p227) with photographs of Ross and Kidderminster. In the May 1988 edition of the Railway Magazine (p284) there is a photograph and description of Kidderminster as this station won the British Rail Award for the most meritous entry in the volunteer section of the Railway Heritage Awards for 1987.

CHAPTER NINE

The Opening of the Railway
- as seen through the eyes of a Ross Gazette Reporter

This report of the opening of the Ross and Monmouth Railway appeared in the August 7th. 1873 edition of the Ross Gazette. The author was given this report by Mr. Nigel Heins who had laboriously copied it out by hand. Mr. Heins was a reporter on the Ross Gazette when the first edition of this book was published and was a source of information and names of informants. Permission to reprint this was freely given by the former Editor of the paper.

"It is with much pleasure we have to chronicle the opening of the Ross and Monmouth Railway, which took place on Monday last and, in doing so, we have to congratulate the promoters of the line and all those who have aided towards its present state of completion.

The line, as many of our readers are aware, was announced to be opened on Friday last, and many people who yield to that proverbial ill-luck attendant on schemes and plans arranged for that ill-omened day, shrugged their shoulders when they saw the placards issued containing the announcement. Singular there was a hitch, and superstition held up its head for the nonce. We may explain the mishap, by stating that on Thursday last, the Government Inspector of Railways, Colonel Rich, officially inspected the line in company with Colonel Vaughan, Mr. Henry Minett, Mr. J.E.S. Hewett and Mr. Firbank jun. To these gentlemen, most of the credit is due for the origination and construction of the line. There was also present Mr. Burlinson (Superintendent of the G.W.R.), Mr. Armstrong (Engineer of the G.W.R.), Mr. Owen (Engineer), Mr. Elliott, Mr. Stennett and others interested in the day's proceedings. Col. Rich made a careful scrutiny of the whole line - travelling on foot through the tunnels and ascertaining that all arrangements at the various stations were efficient.

Much attention and time was devoted to the important work of testing the bridges, these being crossed and re-crossed with the full weight at command several times. After the gallant Colonel had pointed out a few requirements, and made one or two suggestions, he expressed himself pleased with what he saw, and sanctioned the opening of the line. Large posting bills and timetables, which had previously been prepared, were issued the same evening; but later on in the day, however, Col. Rich appears to have discovered that there was no turntable at the Monmouth end, for the purpose of reversing the engine to enable it to perform the return journey in its natural position, with tender behind instead of in front as would have been the case under the existing circumstances. This he considered a drawback, as the tender in front of the engine would necessarily hinder the look-out of the driver, and might be the means of an accident, so he countermanded his former dictum and forbade the opening of the line until the difficulty was obviated. The announcement of the opening not being made till late in the evening, and after the event being still later, the crowd that assembled at Ross Station with the intention of going on the first train (8.45 a.m.) were unaware of anything wrong until they were told that the train could not start, but that the difficulty might be bridged over before the time set down for the next train (11.47). Nothing deterred, a large number assembled at the latter hour and were again doomed to disappointment by being told that no trains would run that week. No time, however, was lost and after several communications had passed between the managers and Col. Rich, permission was given to use what is called a tank engine, which dispenses with the necessity for a tender.

On Saturday, it was reported that the line would really be open on Monday morning in accordance with the time-tables issued, and to re-assure the public the Town Crier was sent round early on Monday morning with the sweeping confirmation of the report. About seven minutes behind time, a well-filled train, consisting of eight carriages, steamed out of the station in the tamest manner, not a drum being heard, nor a flag unfurled to mark the auspicious event. If it was tame, it was soon shown that there was business meant and the officials at the stations on route were civil, prompt and energetic. Long may this be so! The travelling was remarkably easy and smooth. We have only one suggestion to make - our remembrance of the first trip being so gratifying, we cannot complain, we only suggest - and that is that the distance from Tudorville to Ross Station is somewhat long, the Company should erect, if not a station, at least a platform for the convenience of the colony of Ashfield, Tudorville, Archenfield and the surrounding places. The Company would find a good return at the rate of 2d. or 3d. for the journey (third-class) which no one would grumble to pay. The line, we are informed, is twelve and a half miles in length from the station at Ross to Wyebridge, Monmouth. It was commenced in the Autumn of 1868, on the Ross side, and the operations were confined to the portion of the line between this town and Kerne Bridge for the first two years. Then there was an interval of a year in which there was a cessation of work; consequently the line as far as completed will have been nearly four years in hand. There are two tunnels, the principal of which is at Coppet Wood and is 628 yards in length. The second tunnel runs under Symonds Yat, is cut through solid rock and is a quarter of a mile in extent. The time occupied in the boring of the tunnels was eighteen months. At the Coppet Cutting the operation was commenced at each end and the boring parties met in the centre of the tunnel within an inch - a very creditable feat of engineering skill. At each end of the tunnels, as may be supposed, there is some heavy open cutting and beyond this the groundwork has been of an ordinary character. Three bridges, however, will span the Wye in connection with the line. Two of these, of elegant construction, form part of the route completed, one being at Kerne Bridge, and the other at Stowfield. The former is 330 ft., has a centre span of 150 ft. and a span on each side of 62 ft. Of stations there are four, including that at Wye Bridge viz., Symonds Yat, the Severn and Wye Valley Junction at Lydbrook and Kerne Bridge. The permanent stations are built of old red sandstone, obtained from Tudorville and have a neat and substantial appearance. At the Kerne Bridge a diversion of the turnpike road, as at Monmouth, had to be made, and a great deal more work has had to be performed than had been anticipated in the original scheme in this kind of work. The line of railway runs by the side of the River Wye nearly all the way, and thus the advantages of the "Wye Tour" are partially secured to the railway passengers. If the Company will only provide a few open carriages they will prove of great utility and make the line all the more popular. There is no prettier scenery in England than is to be found between Lydbrook Station (Severn and Wye Junction) and Monmouth. It is impossible for the pen to do justice to the loveliness of the ever-varying, ever lovely scene. On each side of the river there is a diversity of hill and dale, with thickly wooded plantations. Massive rocks stand out in bold relief partially robed and fringed with various kinds of trees, ferns and vegetation common to the district. The rockwork assumes numerous fantastic, castellated, stately shapes, defying accurate description, although the glorious picture lingers in the mind's eye with pleasurable intensity. The Doward, the Drooping Wells, the "Three Sisters", Symonds Yat, all have their peculiar charms. Passing the Coldwell Rocks and getting in sight of the Leys, the residence of J.M. Bannerman, Esq., a change in the panoramic landscape occurs, and the eye dwells with rapture on the sylvan spot, regretful that the speed of the train should so soon put an end to the gratification. The journey ends at Wye Bridge, Monmouth where a temporary station has been erected. It is the intention of the Company to complete the line in course of a short time as far as Troy. This will necessitate the completion of the third bridge across the river. Persons journeying from the temporary station for South Wales and vice versa can be conveyed through the town, from one station to another, by omnibus for about the same fare as that charged from the Troy terminus at present into Monmouth, whilst visitors to the town will only have a few yards to walk to be in the centre of it. On the occasion of our visit, the Monmouth folks appeared to be smarting under the disappointment of the previous Friday and little or no notice having been given that there was to be no mistake this time, they were unaware for the most part that trains were really to run on Monday. It was the tale of the wolf over again. Consequently there was but a small number of passengers travelling on the return journey to Ross. Many passengers, however, were picked up at the intervening stations. There was no demonstration or attempt at anything of the kind if we except a flag hung out at Kerne Bridge Station and a cheer raised by some boys in the train when at Lydbrook. It may be a simple matter to record, but we may as well mention it in the absence of events of greater moment:- our townsman Mr. Joseph Turnock, was fortunate in securing the first 1st. Class ticket from Ross to Monmouth and the first from Monmouth to Ross. These tickets he will be allowed to keep as relics of the day. We should add that the stations at Kerne Bridge and Symonds Yat are very convenient - that at the latter place being constructed with an idea of the probably greater influx of visitors that will occasionally occur. We cannot conclude our notice without expressing our earnest hope for the success and prosperity of the line, both on account of the benefit it will confer on the town and to the reward, the pluck and perseverance of the original promoters. That the railway may enjoy a long and safe career of usefulness, adding its strong yet ornate link to the chain of important commercial enterprise, is the sincere wish of the Ross Gazette".

Symonds Yat Station - outline of platform visible

Symonds Yat from line of railway

A NOSTALGIC JOURNEY

These details were given to the author by Mr. Martin Morris, a former Chief Reporter of the Ross Gazette.

BRITISH RAILWAYS
(Western Region)

SPECIAL "LAST TRAIN"

CHEPSTOW - MONMOUTH - ROSS-ON-WYE - CHEPSTOW

ALSO TOUR TO

SUDBROOK PUMPING STATION

ARRANGED FOR MEMBERS OF THE

STEPHENSON LOCOMOTIVE SOCIETY (MIDLAND AREA)

SUNDAY, 4th. JANUARY, 1959

	ARRIVE	DEPART
Chepstow		11.20 a.m.
Tintern	11.35 a.m.	11.45 a.m.
Redbrook-on-Wye	12.05 p.m.	12.15 p.m.
Monmouth (Troy)	12.22 p.m.	12.40 p.m.
Symonds Yat	12.55 p.m.	1.05 p.m.
Lydbrook Jcn.	1.10 p.m.	1.20 p.m.
Ross-on-Wye	1.36 p.m.	1.55 p.m.
Monmouth (Troy)	2.15 p.m.	2.30 p.m.
Chepstow	3.13 p.m.	3.20 p.m.
Caldicot Jcn.	3.30 p.m.	3.40 p.m.
Sudbrook Pumping Station	3.50 p.m.	5.10 p.m.
Severn Tunnel Junction	5.25 p.m.	

NOTES

1. Rail services to Chepstow to connect with the special train will be available as follows:-

Bristol (Temple Meads)	depart	9.00 a.m.
Birmingham (Snow Hill)	depart	9.00 a.m.) calling specially at
Gloucester (Central)	depart	10.30 a.m.) Chepstow to set down
Cardiff (General)	depart	10.25 a.m.) passengers for the tour.
Newport	depart	10.42 a.m.)

2. Participants travelling from Gloucester (Central), Cardiff (General) and Newport can obtain Second Class Day Excursion tickets to Chepstow (available for return from Severn Tunnel Junction) for 5/6d., 4/-d and 2/9d. respectively UPON PRODUCTION OF SPECIAL TOUR TICKET at Station Booking Offices.

3. A Booking Office will be provided on the train from Chepstow for the issue of local tickets of souvenir value.

4. Return services available from Severn Tunnel Junction are:-

5.38 p.m.	for	Newport and Cardiff
5.48 p.m.	for	Bristol (Stapleton Road)
6.05 p.m.	for	Bristol (Stapleton Road and Temple Meads)
6.22 p.m.	for	Gloucester (Central) and Birmingham (Snow Hill)

    (Change at Gloucester for Birmingham)

5. Members may retain their tickets as souvenirs.

    The Stephenson Locomotive Society announce:-

    a) Any member unable to use his Tour Ticket MUST return it to the Area Secretary to reach him at least one clear day before the Tour.

    b) Members from Birmingham are reminded that 'bus services from suburbs to the City run at half-hourly intervals on Sunday mornings.

    c) Tea and light refreshments will be available on the train from Chepstow.

    d) The Monmouth Local History Society will provide an Exhibition at Troy Station, depicting early Railway schemes of the area and other items of Railway interest.

JOTTINGS FROM THE ROSS GAZETTE

December 18th. 1920

Presentations were made to Mr. C.J. Rees who retired as stationmaster at Ross after 47 years service with the Great Western Railway.

December 26th. 1929

Stones believed to have been place by children on the Ross-Monmouth railway line between Symonds Yat and Lydbrook caused the derailment of a gangers' motor trolley.
One of the two men on the trolley suffered a fractured ankle, a lacerated scalp and slight concussion.

January 23rd. 1931

Yat Rocks Danger

Following the crash of a boulder weighing several tons from the cliffs at Symonds Yat on to the railway line, causing the derailment of a passenger train, an examination of the cliffs disclosed that there were thousands of tons of rock which had become loosened and which presented a real danger.
The Great Western Railway Company were taking remedial action.

THIS AND THAT

Carriers on the line were :-

Foster's Parcel Express (c1890 - c 1914)
Sutton & Co. Ltd. (c 1880 - ?)
R.T. Smith & Co. (dates unknown)

The Line's horse drawn predecessor was the 'Royal Mail' which ran from the Royal Hotel Ross, to Monmouth, Chepstow etc. daily at 10 a.m., 2 p.m. and 4.30 p.m.

When the line was running, omnibuses owned by the principal Ross hotels left Ross Station after the arrival of each train to any part of the

The Line was used annually by the Ross Sunday Schools for their 'Bun Fight' at Goodrich Court.

The famous Rolls family in Monmouth held a big party for their son's 'Coming of Age'. For three days the Line offered cheap fares to Monmouth. This was their time-table :-

	p.m.	p.m.	returning p.m.
Ross	2.45	7.00	Troy 11.00
Kerne Bridge	2.55	7.10	May Hill 11.05
Lydbrook Junction	3.00	7.16	

Symonds Yat Station - outline of platforms visible

The railway alongside the River Wye.

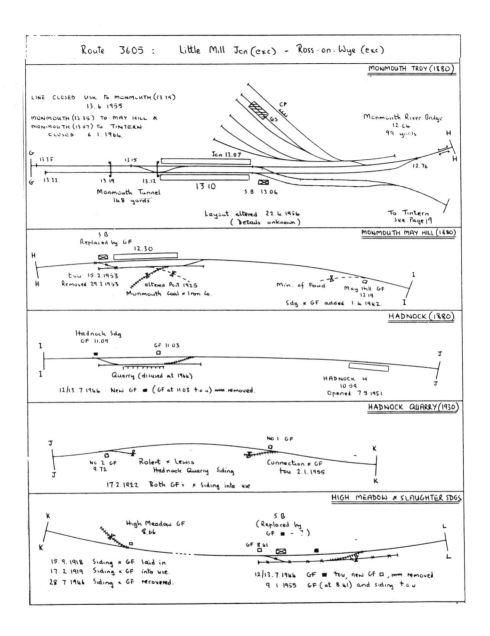

Route 3605 :   Little Mill Jcn (exc) - Ross-on-Wye (exc)

MONMOUTH TROY (1880)

LINE CLOSED USK to MONMOUTH (13.15)
13.6 1955

MONMOUTH (13.35) TO MAY HILL &
MONMOUTH (13.07) TO TINTERN
CLOSED   6.1.1964.

Monmouth River Bridge
12.64
99 yards

G
13.35   13.15   Jcn 13.07
G
13.32   13.19   13.12   13.10   5.B 13.06

12.76

Monmouth Tunnel
148 yards

Layout altered 22.4.1956
(Details unknown)

To Tintern
See Page 19

MONMOUTH MAY HILL (1880)

S.B
Replaced by GF
12.30

H
tou 15.2.1953
H   Removed 29.3.1953   altered Post 1925
Munmouth Coal & Iron Co.

Min. of Food.   May Hill GF
12.19

Sdg & GF added 1.4.1942.

I

HADNOCK (1880)

Hadnock Sdg
GF 11.09   GF 11.03

I
I   Quarry (disused at 1964)   HADNOCK H   J
10.59   J
12/13.7.1944   New GF ■ (GF at 11.03 t.o.u.) ⊢⊢⊢ removed.   Opened 7.9.1951

HADNOCK QUARRY (1930)

No 1 GF

J   K
No 2 GF   Robert & Lewis   K
J   9.72   Hadnock Quarry Siding   Connection & GF
tou 2.1.1955

17.2.1922   Both GF's & Siding into use

HIGH MEADOW & SLAUGHTER SDGS

K   S.B   L
High Meadow GF   (Replaced by
8.66   GF ■ - ?)
K   GF 8.41   L
15.9.1918   Siding & GF laid in
17.2.1919   Siding & GF into use.   12/13.7.1944   GF ■ tou, new GF □, ⊢⊢⊢ removed.
28.7.1946   Siding & GF recovered.   9.1.1955   GF (at 8.41) and siding t.o.u

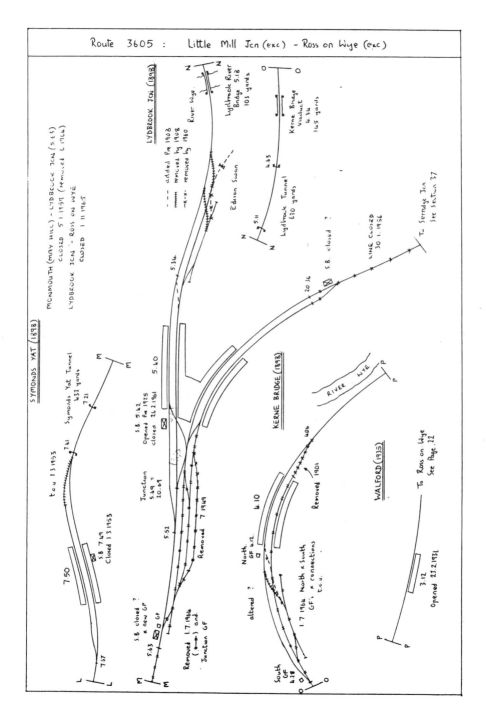

Route 3605 : Little Mill Jcn (exc) - Ross on Wye (exc)

MONMOUTH (MAY HILL) - LYDBROOK JCN (5 & 5)
CLOSED 5.1.1959 (REMOVED 6.1964)
LYDBROOK JCN - ROSS ON WYE
CLOSED 1.11.1965

SYMONDS YAT (1898)

LYDBROOK JCN (1898)

KERNE BRIDGE (1898)

WALFORD (1935)

43

FURTHER READING

Track Layout Diagrams of the G.W.R. & B.R.W.R. Section 36 - R.A. Cooke
Forgotten Railways - South Wales - James Page
Monmouths Railways - W.J.P. Shirehampton, M.A.
The Book of Ross-on-Wye - Martin Morris
A Good Plain Country Town - Fred Druce
Kelly's Directory, Jakeman & Carvers Directory & Littlebury's Directory.

The Dean Forest Railway Society (Norchard, Forest of Dean) and the G.W.R. Museum, (Coleford), are worth visiting for memorabilia of the Ross & Monmouth Railway as well as other railway miscellania.

Symonds Yat, R Wye

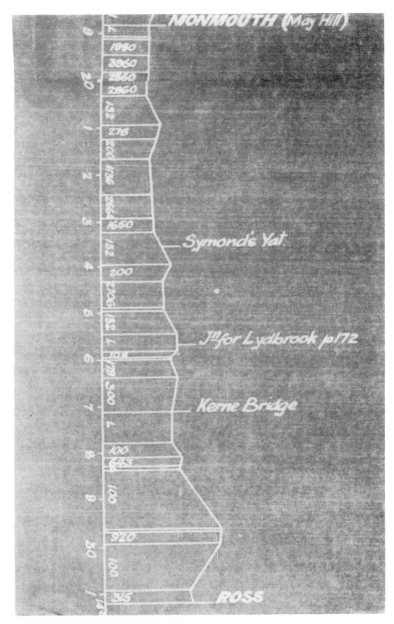

Gradients on the Ross & Monmouth Railway.